# YOUTUBE MASTERY:

## The Ultimate Guide to Launching Your Channel

## QASI JAMES

**YOUTUBE MASTERY: THE ULTIMATE GUIDE TO
LAUNCHING YOUR CHANNEL**

**YOUTUBE MASTERY: THE ULTIMATE GUIDE TO LAUNCHING YOUR CHANNEL**

TABLE OF CONTENTS

## Contents

**YOUTUBE MASTERY: THE ULTIMATE GUIDE TO LAUNCHING YOUR CHANNEL**

**YOUTUBE MASTERY: THE ULTIMATE GUIDE TO LAUNCHING YOUR CHANNEL**

# INTRODUCTION

Creating a YouTube channel is an exciting journey that lets you share your creativity, knowledge, and passion with an international audience. This part presents the aide and establishes the vibe for the per user's investigation into the universe of YouTube.

## 1.1 Why Start a YouTube Channel?

Beginning a YouTube channel offers various advantages and valuable open doors. This part investigates the inspirations driving making a channel, like individual articulation, sharing skill, constructing a local area, or in any event, chasing after a lifelong in satisfied creation.

**YOUTUBE MASTERY: THE ULTIMATE GUIDE TO LAUNCHING YOUR CHANNEL**

## 1.2 Advantages of Having a YouTube Channel

Detail the different benefits that accompany having a YouTube channel. This could incorporate contacting a wide crowd, constructing an individual brand, potential for adaptation, organizing valuable open doors, and the opportunity to add to an energetic web-based local area.

## 1.3 Is YouTube Ideal for You?

Help peruses in surveying whether YouTube lines up with their objectives and interests. Address factors like time responsibility, content creation abilities, and the capacity to deal with expected difficulties. This segment intends to assist peruses with coming to an educated conclusion about whether beginning a YouTube channel is the ideal decision for them.

Make sure to urge peruses to ponder their exceptional assets and interests as they leave on this innovative and possibly remunerating venture.

# 2. Arranging Your YouTube Channel

Prior to jumping into content creation, it's urgent to have a thoroughly examined plan for your YouTube channel. This segment guides you through the underlying arranging stages to guarantee major areas of strength for a.

## 2.1 Define Your Niche

Developing a targeted and engaged audience necessitates locating a niche. Investigate your inclinations, mastery, and what separates you from others. This segment assists you with reducing your substance center, guaranteeing that your channel has an exceptional offer.

**YOUTUBE MASTERY: THE ULTIMATE GUIDE TO LAUNCHING YOUR CHANNEL**

## 2.2 Recognizing Your Main interest group

Understanding your main interest group is critical to making content that reverberates. Characterize the segment and psychographic qualities of your optimal watchers. Investigate how your substance can address their necessities, interests, and difficulties.

## 2.3 Contender Investigation

Examining contenders can give important experiences into effective procedures and content holes. This section shows you how to do a thorough competitor analysis, helping you figure out what works in your niche and where you can be unique.

## 2.4 Defining Objectives for Your Channel

Laying out clear objectives provides your channel bearing and motivation. Whether it's arriving at a specific number of endorsers, perspectives, or cultivating local area commitment, this part assists you with defining practical and quantifiable objectives for present moment and long haul achievement.

By completely arranging your YouTube channel, you improve the probability of making content that resounds with your crowd and lines up with your all-encompassing targets. This makes way for a more vital and satisfying substance creation venture.

# 3. Creating a YouTube Account

The first step in establishing your presence on YouTube is to create an account. This segment guides you through the most common way of setting up your record and advancing it for your image.

## 3.1 Pursue a Google Record

To get to YouTube, you'll require a Google account. This part gives a bit by bit guide on making a Google account on the off chance that you don't as of now have one. It underlines the significance of utilizing an expert email address related with your channel's substance.

## 3.2 Making a YouTube Channel

When you have a Google account, you can make your YouTube channel. This segment makes sense of the various choices for channel types (individual, business, or brand) and finds a way you through the ways to set up your channel name, profile picture, and cover workmanship.

## 3.3 Modifying Your Channel Settings

Modifying your channel settings makes a firm and marked look. This part investigates the different customization choices accessible, including channel format, highlighted areas, and connections to virtual entertainment. It likewise covers the significance of making a convincing "About" segment that acquaints your channel with possible watchers.

By following these means, you'll lay out areas of strength for a for your YouTube channel, making it outwardly engaging and adjusting it to your substance and brand character. Modifying your channel guarantees that watchers have a positive initial feeling when they visit your page.

# 4. Making Your YouTube Channel Memorable and Recognizable

It is Essential to Establish a Strong Brand Presence This segment centers around key components of marking to give your channel an expert and strong look.

## 4.1 How to Create a Channel Logo

A channel logo is a picture of your brand. This part gives direction on planning a logo that mirrors the subject and character of your substance. It covers angles like variety decision, typography, and effortlessness to guarantee your logo is effectively conspicuous across various stages.

## 4.2 Channel Flag and Work of art

The channel flag and work of art assume a critical part in making an outwardly engaging and strong brand. This part makes sense of the ideal aspects for pennants and offers tips on making convincing fine art that lines up with your substance and specialty. It accentuates the significance of refreshing pennants to reflect changes in your substance or marking.

## 4.3 Making a Convincing Channel Depiction

Your channel depiction is an amazing chance to acquaint yourself with expected endorsers. This part directs you through the method involved with creating a convincing feed portrayal that gives an unmistakable outline of your substance, exhibits your character, and urges watchers to buy in. It likewise covers the utilization of watchwords to upgrade discoverability.

By zeroing in on these marking components, you'll make a channel that sticks out and has an enduring effect on your crowd. A very much planned logo, flag, and channel portrayal add to the general incredible skill and engaging quality of your YouTube image.

## 5. Setting Up Your Equipment

To produce videos of high quality, you need the right tools. This part directs you through the fundamental parts of setting up your recording stuff to guarantee proficient looking and sounding substance.

### 5.1 Choosing the Right Camera

In order to produce high-quality videos, selecting the right camera is an essential step. This part examines contemplations, for example, camera types (DSLRs, mirror less, or cell phones), goal, outline rates, and elements. Additionally, it gives people just starting out options that are affordable.

## 5.2 Sound Gear

Great sound quality is similarly significant as video quality. This part investigates receiver choices, including USB and XLR mouthpieces, lavaliere amplifiers, and shotgun mouthpieces. It talks about how important it is to reduce background noise and gives advice on how to get clear and crisp audio.

## 5.3 Lighting Arrangement

Legitimate lighting improves the general look of your recordings. This segment digs into the significance of lighting, regular versus counterfeit light, and three-point lighting arrangements. It offers advice on how to position lights to get the best results and suggests inexpensive lighting equipment.

## 5.4 Stabilization and Tripods

Stable footage is necessary for a professional appearance. This part talks about the significance of mounts and adjustment gadgets for cameras or cell phones. It investigates various kinds of mounts, gimbals, and stabilizers, giving proposals in light of your shooting needs.

By getting it and putting resources into the right gear, you'll be exceptional to deliver top notch recordings that dazzle your crowd. Whether you're on a careful spending plan or searching for further developed choices, this segment assists you with pursuing informed choices for your particular substance creation necessities.

# 6. Making your most huge Video

Since you have your gear set up, right now is the ideal entryway to plunge into the inventive movement of making your most basic video. This segment gives a bit by bit manual for help you in making, altering, and organizing your presentation video.

## 6.1 Coordinating Your Substance

Prior to creating a ruckus all through town button, watchful organizing guarantees your substance is connecting with and particularly planned. Conceptualizing thoughts, picking a theme that lines up with your channel's claim to fame, and making a video system are completely shrouded in this part. It highlights the importance of a persuading opening and an unquestionable wellspring of motivation.

## 6.2 Setting up and Illustrating

Making a substance or blueprint is essential for remaining mindful of spotlight and passing on a sound message. This section explains how to write engaging scripts, including how to use storytelling techniques, keep a conversational tone, and make sure everything is clear. Also, it examines the harmony among abruptness and content that has been coordinated.

## 6.3 Shooting Strategies Successful

Shooting methods can fundamentally improve your accounts' visual allure. This part covers stray pieces like showing, strategy, and camera centers. Besides, it discusses the importance of staying in contact with the camera, changing the receptiveness, and reducing establishment interferences.

## 6.4 Video Changing Wanderer pieces

Changing is where your harsh film changes into a cleaned video. This part presents essential video changing considerations and programming choices. This section covers adding music or voiceovers, consolidating changes, cutting and organizing cuts, and enhancing your video's overall visual appeal. In a similar vein, strategies are provided for maintaining a solid modifying style.

# 7. Working on Your Accounts for Search

Making inconceivable substance is only significant for the circumstance; Enhancing your recordings for search makes them easier to find. This part guides you through the crucial phases of site smoothing out (Website improvement) on YouTube.

## 7.1 Watchword Investigation

Understanding the watchwords your vested party is searching for is urgent. This part examines mechanical assemblies and strategies for expression research, helping you with perceiving significant and high-situating watchwords for your video content.

It highlights the meaning of using watchwords regularly in your substance.

## 7.2 Creating Captivating Titles

Your video's title should be catchy and full of keywords because it is the first thing viewers see. This section offers advice on how to create catchy titles that accurately represent your content. For improved hunt perceivability, it investigates the ideal length and design of titles.

## 7.3 Composing Portrayals and Labels

Search rankings are intensely affected by the video depiction and labels. This portion guides you through forming informational and watchword rich video portrayals. It in like manner gets a handle on the meaning of using significant marks and how to definitively put them to work on your video's discoverability.

## 7.4 Thumbnail Design Tips

An eye-getting thumbnail urges clients to tap on your video. This fragment covers thumbnail setup best chips away at, including the usage of incredible pictures, consistent stamping, and interfacing with visuals. It highlights the meaning of making thumbnails that exactly address your video content.

You can expand your possibilities contacting a bigger crowd by upgrading your recordings for web crawlers. These methodologies help your accounts with surfacing in question things and attract watchers who are really enthusiastic about your substance. Make a point to stay consistent with your smoothing out tries for each video you disperse.

# 8. Transferring and Distributing

When your video is prepared, the transferring and distributing process is urgent for amplifying its deceivability and commitment. This part directs you through the means of transferring, setting protection choices, and enhancing key components.

## 8.1 Transferring Your Video

Transferring your video to YouTube includes something other than choosing a record. The technical aspects of uploading, such as supported file formats, video resolution settings, and uploading from various devices, are covered in this section. Additionally, it emphasizes the significance of customizing the video thumbnail.

## 8.2 Choosing Privacy Settings for Your Video

Choose the privacy settings that best control your video's visibility. The distinctions between videos that are public, private, and unlisted are clarified in this section. It additionally covers contemplations for booking video discharges and the effect of protection settings on search deceivability.

## 8.3 Thumbnails, Titles, and Depictions

Streamline the last subtleties prior to hitting distribute. This segment supports the significance of convincing thumbnails and guides you through the method involved with picking the right one. To get the most out of search visibility and viewer engagement, it also revisits the creation of captivating titles and descriptions packed with keywords.

## 8.4 Booking Recordings

Timing is pivotal for arriving at your interest group. This part gives bits of knowledge into booking your video discharges for ideal watcher commitment. It clarifies how for utilize YouTube's booking component and contemplations for various time regions.

By focusing on these subtleties during the transferring and distributing process, you'll expand the possibilities of your video being found and delighted in by your ideal interest group. Make sure to be steady in your transfer timetable to construct expectation and dependability among your watchers.

## 9. Developing Your Crowd

Constructing and drawing in with your crowd is a vital part of an effective YouTube channel. This section focuses on ways to connect with your audience, collaborate with others, and expand your reach.

### 9.1 Advancing Your Recordings via Online Entertainment

Expand your range past YouTube by advancing your recordings via online entertainment stages. This part gives tips on making shareable substance, using different virtual entertainment channels, and creating connecting with subtitles and presents on direct people to your YouTube recordings.

**YOUTUBE MASTERY: THE ULTIMATE GUIDE TO LAUNCHING YOUR CHANNEL**

## 9.2 Joint efforts and Cross-Advancement

Joint efforts can open your channel to new crowds. This part investigates the advantages of teaming up with other <u>YouTubers</u> and powerhouses in your specialty. It gives direction on moving toward expected partners, arranging joint activities, and actually cross-advancing each other's substance.

## 9.3 Drawing in with Your Watchers

Building areas of strength for a require dynamic commitment. This part talks about the significance of answering remarks, requesting watcher input, and gathering information or overviews. It likewise covers methodologies for making a feeling of local area through live visits, interactive discussions, and local area posts.

## 9.4 Answering Remarks

Drawing in with your crowd through remarks is essential for building a faithful following. This segment gives direction on answering remarks really, cultivating a positive and comprehensive local area, and taking care of useful analysis. It stresses the significance of viewer interaction in fostering loyalty and trust.

By executing these crowd development systems, you'll draw in new watchers as well as make a strong local area around your substance. Effectively captivating with your crowd encourages a feeling of association, which can prompt expanded viewership and supported accomplishment for your YouTube channel.

## 10. Systems for Adaptation

For some YouTubers, transforming their enthusiasm into a type of revenue is a huge achievement. From joining YouTube's Accomplice Program to exploring outside income streams through sponsorships, brand arrangements, product, and subsidiary advertising, this segment inspects different adaptation methodologies.

### 10.1 YouTube Associate Program

Transforming into a YouTube Associate grants you to get cash clearly from YouTube through advancement pay. The prerequisites, application interaction, and qualification rules are laid out in this section. Moreover, it talks about

YouTube's different promotion configurations and income age systems.

## 10.2 Partnerships with Brands and Sponsorships

Forming partnerships with brands and obtaining sponsorships can be productive ways to generate revenue. Tracking down pertinent backers, arranging bargains, and keeping up with legitimacy in supported content are totally canvassed in this part. It similarly covers the meaning of agreeing with brands that reverberate with your group.

## 10.3 Item and Part Displaying

Expand your revenue streams by exploring stock arrangements and auxiliary advancing. This part looks at the pushes toward make and sell stock through stages like YouTube Product Rack. It furthermore explores accomplice publicizing, where you secure commissions by propelling things or organizations through stand-out part joins.

By joining these variation procedures, you can make a sensible compensation from your YouTube channel. It's basic to discover some sort of congruity among transformation and staying aware of the trust of your group. Straightforwardness and validness are basic to ensuring that your transformation attempts overhaul rather than cut down the watcher experience.

# 11. Exploring Your Channel Execution

Understanding how your channel is performing is dire for chasing after informed decisions and further developing your substance method. This portion jumps into utilizing YouTube Examination to properly follow key estimations and change your procedure.

## 11.1 An Outline of YouTube Investigation

YouTube Examination offers valuable experiences into the presentation of your channel. This part gives a blueprint of the YouTube Assessment dashboard, figuring out the different regions and estimations open. It underlines the meaning of regularly looking at examination to assess the sufficiency of your substance and group responsibility.

## 11.2 Following Key Estimations

Perceive and follow key execution estimations to measure the result of your accounts and for the most part channel. This section covers crucial estimations, for instance, sees, watch time, ally improvement, dynamic clicking factor (CTR), and swarm economics. It provides guidance on unraveling these estimations and sorting out their ideas for your channel.

## 11.3 Changing Your Philosophy considering Assessment

Examination data enlightens key decisions. This part guides you through the strategy engaged with using assessment to recognize designs, handle swarm lead, and seek after data driven decisions. It discusses how to utilize YouTube Examination to change your substance methodology, posting timetable, and commitment endeavors.

Regularly separating your channel's show licenses you to refine your procedure, recognize what resonates with your group, and smooth out for advancement. By staying informed about your examination, you can seek after informed decisions to constantly improve and foster your substance strategy.

# 12. Managing Difficulties

Exploring difficulties is an inescapable piece of being a substance maker on YouTube. Problems like copyright concerns, negative feedback, and adapting to algorithm changes are all addressed in this section.

## 12.1 Handling Copyright Matters

Claims regarding copyright can be a significant obstacle for YouTubers. Copyright issues can be understood and navigated with the help of this section. It covers techniques to stay away from copyright encroachment, how to deal with copyright claims, and the significance of utilizing authorized or unique substance.

**YOUTUBE MASTERY: THE ULTIMATE GUIDE TO LAUNCHING YOUR CHANNEL**

## 12.2 Managing Critics and Negative Remarks

Negative remarks and online analysis are difficulties numerous makers face. This part offers techniques for managing critics and negative remarks in a helpful way. It underscores the significance of keeping a positive outlook, directing remarks really, and involving cynicism as a chance for development.

## 12.3 Adjusting to Calculation Changes

YouTube's calculation can go through changes, influencing the deceivability of your substance. This part examines how to adjust to calculation changes by remaining informed about refreshes, grasping positioning elements, and changing your substance methodology in like manner. It underlines the significance of making superior grade, drawing in satisfied that lines up with watcher inclinations.

Effectively exploring these difficulties requires versatility, flexibility, and a proactive way to deal with critical thinking. By tending to copyright concerns, dealing with pessimism successfully, and remaining informed about calculation transforms, you can proceed to develop and flourish as a substance maker on YouTube. Recall that difficulties are essential for the excursion, and figuring out how to beat them adds to long haul achievement.

# 13. Future Development and Broadening

Looking forward and making arrangements for future development is fundamental for the supported outcome of your YouTube channel. This segment investigates methodologies for extending your substance, utilizing different stages, and building a brand past YouTube.

## 13.1 Extending Your Substance

Differentiating your substance can draw in a more extensive crowd and continue to exist watchers locked in. This part talks about ways of extending your substance, including presenting new series, investigating various organizations, teaming up with different makers, and consolidating crowd input. It underscores the significance of remaining consistent with your specialty while advancing with your crowd's advantages.

## 13.2 Taking Advantage of Other Platforms

Although YouTube is a powerful platform, diversifying your online presence can increase your reach. This segment investigates the advantages of utilizing other online entertainment stages, like Instagram, Twitter, TikTok, or an individual blog. It gives advice on how to use cross-promotion strategies and tailor content for each platform.

## 13.3 Structure a Brand Past YouTube

Building a brand stretches out past the substance you make. This segment examines methodologies for building a brand character, including reliable visual components, an unmistakable logo, and a durable web-based presence. It investigates valuable open doors for marketing, making a site, and drawing in with your crowd on an individual level to reinforce your image past the YouTube stage.

By taking into account these development and enhancement systems, you set up for long haul accomplishment as a substance maker. Adjusting to changes, extending your substance contributions, and building areas of strength for a presence across different stages add to a versatile and developing internet based presence.

## 14. CONCLUSION

Congrats on setting out on your YouTube venture! As you finish up this far reaching guide, it's fundamental to think about the vital focus points and the thrilling way forward.

**In this aide, you've learned:**

The inspirations driving beginning a YouTube channel and the advantages it can bring.

The significance of fastidious preparation, including characterizing your specialty, distinguishing your crowd, and defining objectives.

The bit by bit course of making and tweaking your YouTube channel, from planning a logo to creating a convincing channel portrayal.

Setting up and improving your gear for excellent video creation.

The innovative flow of making your most memorable video, from arranging content to video altering fundamentals.

Systems for improving your recordings for search, including watchword examination and thumbnail plan.

putting privacy settings, titles, and descriptions at the forefront when uploading and publishing your videos.

Methods for developing your crowd through web-based entertainment advancement, joint efforts, and drawing in with watchers.

Adaptation techniques, including joining the YouTube Accomplice Program and investigating sponsorships, product, and offshoot promoting.

The significance of dissecting your channel's exhibition utilizing YouTube Examination and changing your methodology in light of bits of knowledge.

Managing normal difficulties, for example, copyright issues, negative remarks, and adjusting to calculation changes.

Making arrangements for future development and enhancement, including extending content, utilizing different stages, and building a brand past YouTube.

As you push ahead, recall that accomplishment on YouTube is an excursion that requires commitment, innovativeness, and flexibility. Remain energetic about your substance, draw in with your crowd, and constantly learn and develop. The YouTube people group is huge and various, and your remarkable voice and point of view can possibly have a significant effect.

I wish you the best of luck as you embark on your YouTube journey! Continue making, associating, and partaking in the thrilling universe of content creation.

### HAPPY JOURNEY

**YOUTUBE MASTERY: THE ULTIMATE GUIDE TO LAUNCHING YOUR CHANNEL**